The World of Insects

INSECTS IN DANGER

Kathryn Smithyman
& Bobbie Kalman

A Crabtree Crown Book

Crabtree Publishing
crabtreebooks.com

INSECTS IN DANGER

Editor-in-Chief Bobbie Kalman

Writing team Kathryn Smithyman, Bobbie Kalman

Editors Kelley MacAulay, Molly Aloian, Robin Johnson

Consultant Patricia Loesche, Ph.D., Animal Behavior Program, Department of Psychology, University of Washington

Design and photo research Margaret Salter

Cover design Margaret Salter

Production manager Candice Campbell

Images Wikimedia Commons: page 6 (top left); all other images: Shutterstock.com

Crabtree Publishing

crabtreebooks.com 800-387-7650

Printed in the U.S.A./CP022026

Published in Canada
Crabtree Publishing
616 Welland Ave.
St. Catharines, Ontario
L2M 5V6

Published in the United States
Crabtree Publishing
347 Fifth Ave
Suite 1402-145
New York, NY 10016

Library and Archives Canada Cataloguing in Publication
Available at the Library and Archives Canada

Library of Congress Cataloging-in-Publication Data
Available at the Library of Congress

Hardcover: 978-1-0398-7309-4
Paperback: 978-1-0398-7367-4
Ebook (pdf): 978-1-0398-7417-6
Epub: 978-1-0398-7466-4

Contents

What are insects?

Insects are **invertebrates**. Invertebrates are animals that do not have **backbones**. A backbone is a row of bones in the middle of an animal's back.

Instead of backbones, insects have **exoskeletons** on the outside of their bodies. An exoskeleton is a hard covering that protects an insect's entire body.

There are millions of ***species****, or types, of insects on Earth. This grasshopper is an insect.*

Three body sections

An insect's body has three main sections: a head, a **thorax**, and an **abdomen**. On its head, the insect has eyes, **mouthparts**, and a pair of **antennae**. The insect uses its antennae to feel, smell, and hear what is around it. The thorax is the middle section of the insect's body. Six legs are attached to the thorax. The abdomen is the rear section of the insect's body. It contains the insect's **organs**.

Many insects have wings. An insect's wings are attached to its thorax.

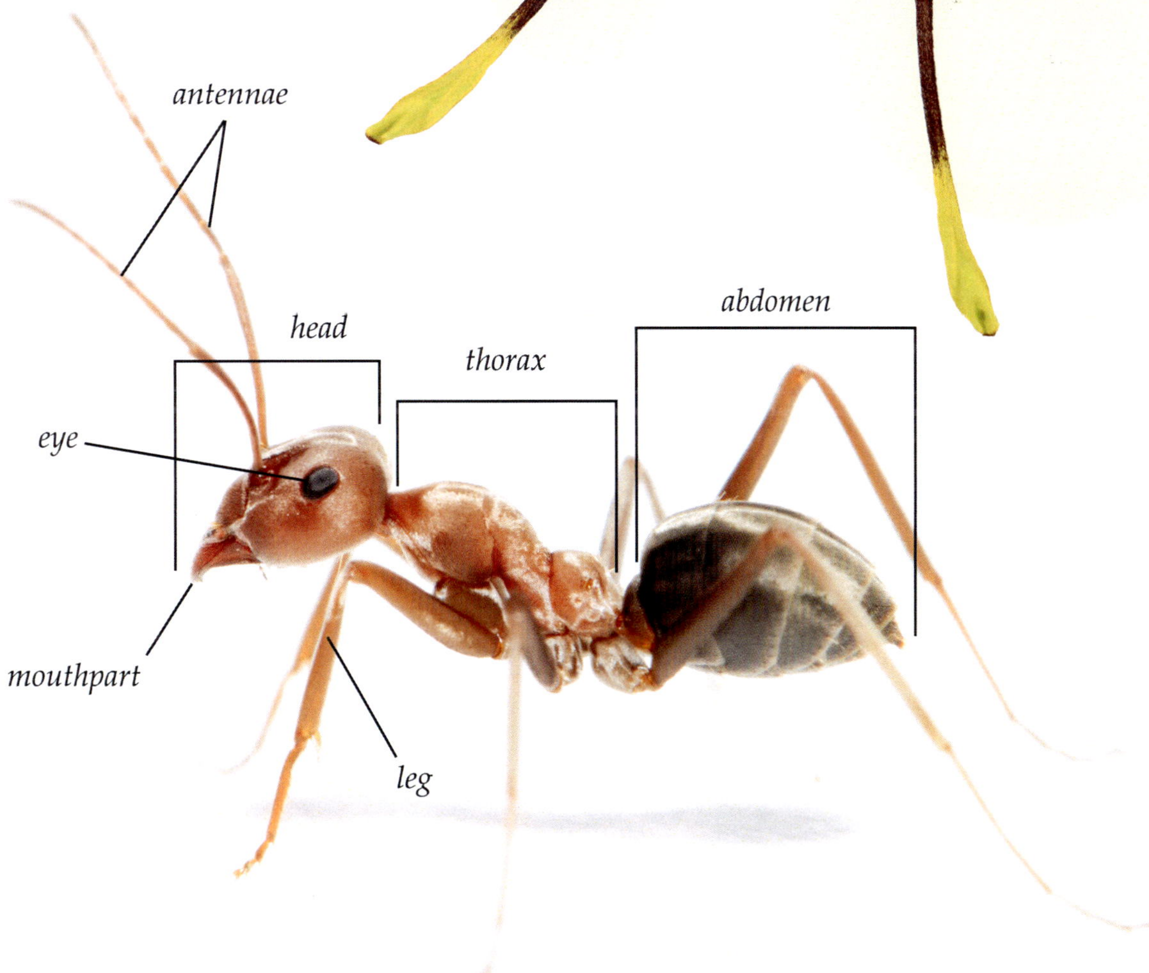

Insects in trouble

Many insects are **endangered**. Endangered animals are at risk of disappearing from Earth forever. Some scientists believe that more insect species will soon become endangered. Many insect species are already **extinct**. Extinct animals no longer live on Earth.

The Xerces Blue butterfly is an extinct insect species.

One species of Australian ant has lived on Earth for millions of years. These ants are called "dinosaur ants" because they have lived on Earth for so long. Dinosaur ants are endangered.

Insect populations

Most people do not realize that some insects are in danger. Many insects have **populations** in the hundreds of thousands! A population is the total number of one species living in an area. An insect species can be endangered even when there are thousands of insects still alive. It is endangered because many insects are often killed at the same time.

Did you know?

Scientists must count insects to find out if their populations are decreasing. Insects are difficult to count, however. Many species fly from place to place. Some insects are tiny or live in places where they are hard to find. Since counting insects is such a challenge, scientists do not always know if insect populations are increasing or decreasing.

Stick insects blend in with the leaves and sticks around them, making it difficult to see and to count them!

Insect habitats

Insects live in many kinds of **habitats**. A habitat is the natural place where an animal or a plant lives. Many insects live in forests, especially in **tropical rain forests**. Insects also live in habitats such as **deserts**, **grasslands**, and **wetlands**.

Thousands of species of insects, including many kinds of beetles, live in tropical rain forests. Tropical rain forests are hot forests that receive a lot of rain.

Deserts are hot, dry habitats. Some species of crickets and ground beetles live in deserts.

Grasslands are flat areas of land, where many grasses grow. Grasshoppers and butterflies live in grasslands.

Wetlands are areas of land that are wet for at least part of the year. Mosquitoes and dragonflies are insects that live in wetlands.

Threats to rainforest insects

Millions of insects live in tropical rain forests. Many kinds of plants grow in these hot, wet habitats. Rainforest insects make homes both on and in the plants. Many insects also eat plant parts, such as seeds, leaves, flowers, and fruits. Some rainforest insects, such as rhinoceros beetles, grow much larger than insects in other habitats do.

The rhinoceros beetle uses the long horn on its head to cut paths through leaves and plants on the rainforest floor.

Cut it out!

Many rainforest insects are in danger. Each day, huge areas of rain forests are **cleared**. To clear an area means to remove all the plants from it. People cut down the trees in rain forests so they can use the wood. When a rain forest is destroyed, many rainforest insects and other animals die.

Rajah Brooke's birdwing butterflies live in rain forests. These insects are endangered because rain forests are being cut down.

Did you know?

Many plants grow close together in rain forests. It is difficult for people to move easily through the forests. As a result, scientists have not yet reached some parts of rain forests. They believe there are many species of rainforest insects that have not yet been discovered. Scientists are worried that some insect species may become extinct before people know they exist!

Harming desert insects

Deserts are dry habitats because they receive little rain. Few plants grow in deserts. Many insects live in deserts, however. Grasshoppers, locusts, and ants are some desert insects.

Some insects, such as harvester ants, live under the ground in deserts to keep cool.

Damaged deserts

Many people also live in deserts. They build cities and **recreational areas** on desert land. When people build in deserts, insects and other animals have less room in which to live and find food.

Not enough water

By building cities in deserts, people put desert insects and other animals in danger. People use a lot of water. They quickly use up the small amount of water in deserts. As a result, desert animals may have trouble finding enough water to survive.

Golf courses are a threat to desert insects. They take up huge areas of land and require a lot of water to stay green.

Grassland insects in trouble

Many types of grasses grow in grasslands. Grasslands are windy, wide-open spaces where few trees grow. Many kinds of insects, including grasshoppers, butterflies, and bees, live in grasslands. Grasshoppers eat grasses. Butterflies and bees drink **nectar** from grassland flowers. Nectar is a sweet liquid found in flowers.

The Dakota skipper can survive only in grasslands. The population of these butterflies is decreasing.

Clearing the land

People are clearing grasslands to plant **crops**. Some grassland insects eat only grassland plants. When people clear grasslands to plant crops, these insect species cannot survive.

Keep off the grass!

People also destroy grasslands when they ride dirt bikes and other vehicles over the land. The dirt bikes rip up the plants. They also ruin the soil so that new plants cannot grow. Without plants and soil, grassland insects have no homes or food.

Grassland insects and other animals are in danger when people clear huge areas of grassland habitats and use them to grow crops.

When people drive their vehicles in grasslands, the tires crush or tear up grassland plants.

Wiping out wetland insects

Wetlands are perfect habitats for **aquatic insects**. Aquatic insects spend all or part of their lives in water. Mayflies, mosquitoes, dragonflies, and certain beetles are aquatic insects. Many wetland insects feed on plants that grow in the water.

Down the drain

All over the world, people are **draining** the water from wetlands. People then build farms, roads, and homes on the land. More than half of the world's wetlands have been drained. When wetlands are drained, wetland insects have no place to live.

Clogged with plants

Some farmers use **fertilizers** on their crops. Fertilizers help plants grow. When it rains, fertilizers can run into wetlands. The fertilizers cause many wetland plants to grow. These new plants grow so close together that they take up all the space and use all the water. Soon, the wetland dries up and many species die.

Pollen carriers

Many insects eat **pollen**. Pollen is a powdery substance found in flowers. To make new flowers, plants need pollen from other plants. As insects eat pollen, some of it sticks to their bodies. When the insects fly or crawl to other plants to find food, they carry the pollen with them on their bodies. Moving pollen from one flower to another is called **pollination**.

Did you know?

Some pollen-eating insects have body parts that help them carry pollen from place to place. For example, honeybees have pockets on their legs for carrying pollen.

Bees are the most common pollinators. Other insects that carry pollen include wasps, moths, butterflies, flies, and beetles.

Crop pollination

Insect pollination helps many kinds of plants grow. Without insects, there would be few trees and flowers. Insects also pollinate crops that people grow for food. Some crops that insects pollinate are apples, almonds, cotton, beans, and pumpkins. Without insects, people would not have many of the foods they eat every day!

Harmful poisons

Many kinds of insects eat crops. To stop insects from eating their crops, many farmers spray the crops with **pesticides**. Pesticides are poisons that kill insects. The pesticide spray not only lands on the crops, it also covers nearby trees, shrubs, and flowers. The pesticides can poison the insects that land on these plants.

Did you know?
Frogs, birds, and other animals eat insects. When these animals eat poisoned insects, the poison gets into their bodies. Insect-eating animals eat a lot of insects! Over time, these animals may also become poisoned.

This man is spraying pesticides on crops.

Pollinators in danger

Many of the insects that are poisoned by pesticides are pollinators, such as bees and butterflies. Without pollinators, most plants cannot make seeds. As a result, fewer plants grow. With fewer plants, fewer insects are able to survive.

Nowhere to live

People also spray poisons on certain plants to kill them. Some of these plants are **host plants**. Host plants are the plants on which some insects lay their eggs. For example, monarch butterflies lay their eggs only on milkweed plants. Many people do not like the look of milkweeds, so they spray poisons on them. Without milkweeds, monarch butterflies have nowhere to lay their eggs.

Honeybees may die when they collect pollen from plants that have been sprayed with pesticides.

Monarch butterflies lay eggs only on milkweeds. The monarch caterpillars that hatch from the eggs eat the host plants.

Insect collecting

Some people collect insects that are beautiful or that look interesting. To collect insects, people capture and kill them. Collectors often pin the insects into **display boxes**.

Collecting is especially harmful to endangered insects. Since the populations of endangered insects are already low, collecting may cause them to become extinct.

These insects are pinned inside a display box.

Did you know?

Collecting is one reason the Apollo butterfly is in danger. Some of these butterflies live high on mountains, whereas others live at the **base**, or bottom, of mountains. Few people climb the mountains to collect Apollo butterflies, but many people collect the butterflies that live at the base of mountains. People have collected so many of these butterflies that the species is now in danger.

Invaders!

People sometimes take plants and animals from one habitat and **introduce** them into other habitats. Many introduced plants and animals spread quickly throughout their new habitats. When introduced plants and animals take over the habitats, they leave no room for **native** plants and animals to live. Native plants and animals are those that first grew or lived in a habitat. They have been in the habitat for a very long time.

Purple loosestrife is an introduced plant that has taken over wetlands across North America. It crowds out many native wetland plants, leaving less food and fewer homes for native wetland animals.

Taking over

Introduced plants and animals that take over a habitat are called **invaders**. Plant invaders kill native plants that some insects need for food. Animal invaders often eat the plants that insects need—or they may even eat the insects themselves!

Did you know?

Wetas are insects that are native to New Zealand. For thousands of years, they had few **predators**. When people first sailed to New Zealand, there were many rats on the ships. The rats escaped and moved onto the land. They became an introduced species in New Zealand. The rats began eating wetas. With rats as predators, wetas are now endangered.

All weta species are in danger. This is a Middle Island tusked weta.

Safe places

People protect insects by protecting insect habitats. Many countries set aside large areas of land, called **preserves**. People are not allowed to destroy plants or harm animals in preserves. People called **rangers** work in preserves to keep the plants and animals safe.

Studying insects

Scientists often study insects in preserves. They also study the plants and animals the insects eat. By studying insects, scientists learn how insects help their habitats. They also find out which insects are in danger. Scientists can then teach people how to protect insects.

Did you know?

Sand dunes are fragile habitats that are destroyed easily. Insects such as northeastern beach tiger beetles live in sand dunes. Fences are being built around sand dunes to keep people off the dunes.

Did you know?

In Africa, endangered elephants and dung beetles live on the same preserves. Elephants make a lot of dung! Dung beetles lay their eggs in dung. The **larvae**, or young insects, that hatch from the eggs feed on the dung. As the larvae feed, they break down the dung into smaller pieces. These smaller pieces become soil. The larvae help keep the preserves clean by breaking down dung.

People can help

Insects are important! To protect insects, people must protect the habitats in which insects live. People can protect forests by using less paper. When people use less paper, they also cut down fewer trees.

Watch out!

Remember that natural areas are home to many insects. When you are walking or biking through these areas, stay on the trails. Riding off the trails kills insects and destroys their homes and sources of food.

People can also help by keeping insect habitats clean.

Building ponds

Students in many schools are helping wetland plants and animals by building ponds. The students study wetlands and then work together to care for the plants and animals that live in their ponds. Caring for ponds helps students learn how important natural wetlands are.

Insect scrapbook

You can help insects by learning more about them. You can start learning about insects in your own yard. Look for insects and watch what they are doing. Take pictures of them. Use the pictures to make a scrapbook. Write one or two sentences about each insect in your book.

Monarchs are my favorite butterflies.

This dragonfly landed on a plant in the park near Grandma's house. It has shiny wings.

I did not get too close to this stinkbug. It was in the garden. Dad sprayed soapy water on it to get it off the plant, but I wouldn't let him kill it.

This is an antlion. It took me a long time to find out what it was called.

Glossary

Note: Boldfaced words that are defined in the text may not appear in the glossary.

crop A group of plants that people grow for food

display box A box that holds items so they can be shown to people

drain To remove water from an area by cutting waterways into the area so that water can flow away

fertilizer A substance that is added to soil to help plants grow

introduce To add a plant or an animal to an area for the first time

organ A part of an animal's body, such as the heart, which does an important job

predator An animal that hunts and eats other animals for food

preserve A place where plants and animals are protected from people's activities, such as collecting

recreational areas Places where people play, such as golf courses and amusement parks

sand dune A mound of sand formed by the wind along a shoreline or in a desert

Index